Presented to the

Franklin Pierce College Library

by
Emily Flint

For Emily Flint,

The Bean & the Scene

With Love & "Respekt",
as my German art
teacher used to say,

Barbara Westman
1976

The Bean & the Scene

DRAWINGS OF BOSTON AND CAMBRIDGE

BY BARBARA WESTMAN

FRANKLIN PIERCE COLLEGE
LIBRARY
RINDGE, NEW HAMPSHIRE

INTRODUCTION

BY HERBERT A. KENNY

1969

BARRE PUBLISHERS

BARRE, MASSACHUSETTS

The people in the pictures are all products of
Barbara Westman's imagination. The Boston Cup,
on the last page, is not. It was originally made
for Boston, England, but somehow wound up here
in the Old State House.

Copyright © 1969 by Barre Publishing Co., Inc.
Library of Congress Card Catalog No. 74-87004
Standard Book Number 8271-6919-1
Design by Klaus Gemming
Printed by Nimrod Press of Boston
Binding by The Sendor Bindery of New York

All rights reserved. Except for use in a review, the
reproduction or utilization of this work in any form
or by any electronic, mechanical, or other means, now
known or hereinafter invented, including photocopying
and recording, and in any information storage and
retrieval system is forbidden without the permission
of the publisher.

Manufactured in the United States of America

INTRODUCTION

If I were the United States Navy I would have Old Ironsides fire a twenty-one gun salute for Barbara Westman. If I were the Governor of Massachusetts I would get bids for inscribing her name in Roman letters around the Golden Dome of the State House. If I were the Mayor of Boston I would hang pennants for her on Bunker Hill Monument, and commission a polychrome statue of her to be erected somewhere in the market district where the most people would see it.

It has long been suspected that I am not the United States Navy, and the latest city and state elections have left me with no authority over affairs of the Commonwealth or its capital. I must then resort to telling you as forcefully as possible how much delight I have taken in the watercolor drawings of Miss Westman, who has caused me, one who loves Boston and Cambridge inordinately, to love them a little more and realize, suddenly and with a sense of euphoria,

how much of their charm I had actually over-looked as I wandered the streets to stop, stare and muse at certain nodal points where the charm intensifies. I have been reborn in her paint box.

Miss Westman, it might as well be acknowledged, is a witch. Fortunately for all of us she is a good witch, who, in a wicked world, a world defeated and depressed, a world running scared and slightly psychopathic, has enough exuberance to save us all. She could, of course, have kept it all to herself and let the rest of us go hang, but good witches (who are also good looking) are not like that. She has let us all in on it. Life is real, life is earnest, life is wonderful! Even lamp-posts and traffic markers which no one has understood since G. K. Chesterton, and little signs in windows which proclaim the very humblest of things, such as "Today's Special, 55 Cents a Pound," are transmogrified by her magic pens and brushes. Transmogrification is what good witches achieve.

Barbara Westman was born in Boston, in the Phillips House of the Massachusetts General Hospital, which, if I am not mistaken, is caught in the corner of one of her paintings, and so she has red salmon brick dust running in her veins. The blood of the Vikings is there also if you are interested in ancestries. She went to Milton High School in Milton, Massachusetts, and Goucher College in Baltimore before her acquisitive eye, which absorbs every detail of a scene, and the itch in her fingers got the best of her and she determined on a career in art. It was perhaps inevitable. Her late father was an architect; her mother was a concert pianist and presently teaches music. Miss Westman's art studies took her to Munich, Germany, and the Malschule Die Form, which was followed by five years at the Museum School in Boston. These were days and nights filled with disciplining, drilling and work. She pieced out her day and her livelihood serving on the information desk at the Museum of Fine Arts. In her fourth and fifth years she taught as well as studied, and, to her delight, won the Ruth Sturdivant Travelling Fellowship, which was to take her back to her beloved Europe.

Off she went to a Europe that was to change her life, for it ultimately enabled her to rediscover America. Afoot and on bicycle she prowled the matrix of our culture—Holland, France, Italy, Spain, Austria, Yugoslavia. Germany she knew. At the end she could cry out, "There isn't a street in Europe that I don't know. I have walked or bicycled down every one." She spent several months painting the Dutch landscape, then three months in Paris drawing and painting the people and the markets. In Rome she had to paint from the housetops because when she tried to work in the streets with easel or scratch pad the men pinched her. She vividly remembers kicking one fresh adolescent. But painting from the *housetops did something for her perspective and her style and the result can be seen in this collection.*

In 1962 she returned, and her travelling fellowship show at the Museum was a success. Then came the letdown. She had emerged into a world indifferent to artists. To support herself, she taught; she took a job as a typist; she painted and prepared for her next exhibit.

"But I was painting Europe from memory," she says, "and it was Ronald Murray, the art director at Houghton Mifflin, who brought me to my senses. 'Where are the people?' he asked, 'Where are the people? Go out and draw people.' I was heart-sick for Europe and those carefree scholarship days. So I went to the North End—there's nothing in Boston more European. Then I saw what I had never seen before—everything I wanted." Barbara Westman had discovered the North End. She went on to discover Beacon Hill (she once lived on Chestnut Street and as a child played in the Public Garden), and, better still, she discovered Harvard Square in Cambridge. "I became a tourist in my own country," she remarks. The Charles had grown as magic as the Seine.

In 1967, the year her father died (surely his gifts show in his daughter's passion for architectural detail), she had her second show, this time at the Wiggin Gallery of the Boston Public Library. In it were drawings and prints as well as paintings, the gleanings of twelve years.

Edgar J. Driscoll, Boston's leading art critic, commented on her exuberance and joie de vivre.

"The lively works on view," he wrote, "reflect her travels and her love of particular places

and people. These range from the activity of Boston's North End and Cambridge's Harvard Square, to Dutch canals and landscape, olive trees in the South of France or the people and mountains of ... Vermont." Exuberance and joie de vivre. True enough; but something bigger and beyond—an idiosyncratic vision of Boston that rises to a pitch of universality. Publisher Alden Johnson sensed this at the exhibition and appealed to Miss Westman to document with her persistent delight more of the Boston and Cambridge that pleased her. This book is the outcome; of the twenty-two reproductions in it, only three were shown at the Wiggin Gallery. The others are new, fired with released creativity, for which Barbara thanks Mr. Johnson and also her latest job as draughtsman-in-residence at the Peabody Museum, Harvard University, a post which leaves her several free days to explain to us in terms of glory the city where she lives, Cambridge, and its parent city, Boston.

Now you know why the Peabody Museum is celebrated by her pen and paints, when one might have expected Memorial Hall, that pleasingly grotesque Harvard emblem. The purpose of art is to show us what we do not see, and we do not

see the Peabody Museum. We may go inside and see the glass flowers but we do not see the undistinguished Victorian compilation of bricks. She shows it to us. On the other hand we do see Hanover Street and The Prato in the North End. As Miss Westman says, "Hanover Street is a great street." She trumpets it in calligraphy on signs in the North End. Indeed it is a great street, and we did not know just how great until Miss Westman jumbled all its people and signs and buildings and boxes into her vibrant painting.

*"This is a people book," she says in triumph,
and looking at her sketches of The Prato
and Hanover Street we know it is. Were any
insensitive soul to remain unconvinced he has only
to look at the Harvard Square paintings.
"Have You Been in Ha-Vahd Squ-Ah-A in the
Sum-mah?" her dancing lettering asks us
and takes us there, and that settles the discussion.
This is a people book. That doesn't prevent it
from being a sign book, because Miss Westman
is quite insane on the subject of signs, nor does it
prevent it from being a historical document.
If the Bayeux Tapestry tells us the technical de-
tails of William the Conqueror's invasion of
England and his conquest better than the
chroniclers of the day, historians are going to turn
to Barbara's drawings for information. So
that's the way it was, eh? Already, the great
Harvard Square street clock is gone, the victim
of an erratic driver. And the traffic officer's
glass booth has vanished. Heigh-ho, the Harvard
Square of July, 1967, has altered in the
Heraclitean flux of time, but not quickly enough
to escape Miss Westman. Time doesn't march
on, if she says, "Wait a minute."*

And her colors! They are the colors I wanted to see, but could not, on Beacon Hill, on Commonwealth Avenue, on Hanover Street, on Chestnut Street, among those Harvard buildings that cluster and parade beyond the Harvard Yard, and the halls and houses in the Harvard Yard. They are, however, the colors that are there and I am now able to see since Miss Westman has said to me, "Of course, that's just the way they are. Look!" Magic! It isn't everyone who can afford a witch; nor every age that can afford a Barbara Westman.

Exuberance, joie de vivre and that delight in detail, that enthusiasm for cornices and crannies, cupolas and crochets, which led Ruskin to write The Stones of Venice, *these are what have made Miss Westman celebrate the red bricks of* Boston and the people that busy the streets *of Boston and Cambridge, Cantabrigian and Bostonian, our brothers, our sisters. And don't forget the dogs. Miss Westman hasn't; they are almost as numerous as the traffic signs. Dogs are dear to her. Traffic signs come to life for her; shop signs come to life for her; everything comes to life for her.*

So, the next time you pass a lamppost say hello to it for her. Now take up her drawings and say hello to Boston and Cambridge, and enjoy and salute Barbara Westman and her happily astigmatic vision of the world.

Herbert A. Kenny

Manchester, Massachusetts, 1969

The Bean & the Scene

The Harvard Lampoon and the Starr Book Shop full of old books.

The Peabody Museum is full of old archaeology and ethnology.

Harvard Square is Harvard Square. There is only one Harvard Square.

Snowfall and sunset over Harvard. The towers of William James,
the Busch-Reisinger Museum and Memorial Hall are against the sky.

This view down over Boston was seen from
the 24th floor of one of the new Prudential Apartments.
That's Beacon Hill over there.

The Burrage House on Commonwealth Avenue was built for
a very wealthy man, to say the least.

The chimney pots in Boston are as interesting as those anywhere.
These are the rooftops of Commonwealth Avenue.

Chestnut Street is just around the corner from Louisburg Square.
The snow is just beginning to come down and you can smell the smoke from the chimney pots.

Barbara Westman

Louisburg Square is the way you really spell it. The brass is always polished on the doorways and the windows are always clean. The lights in the lamps are always lit, and the houses are always very bright. Louis, the dog here, belongs to a lady on the Square. I drew him twice because he roams a lot and I call him "Louis, the King of the Hill."

The dome of the Capitol can be seen from all around.

GOD SAVE THE COMMONWEALTH OF MASSACHUSETTS

The State House was designed by Charles Bulfinch,
the central part with the dome only.
The other parts were added later.
It is perhaps the most delicately designed building
I have seen anywhere.

Flags fly and trees grow and the whole scene sparkles below. This is a drawing
from the balcony outside the Senate Chamber of the Capitol building.

The Athenaeum is a private,
peaceful, sunny place.
The dog, Liberty,
comes every morning
with her mistress.

Barbara Westman

Faneuil Hall is known as "The Cradle of Liberty."
There is a famous golden grasshopper on the top.

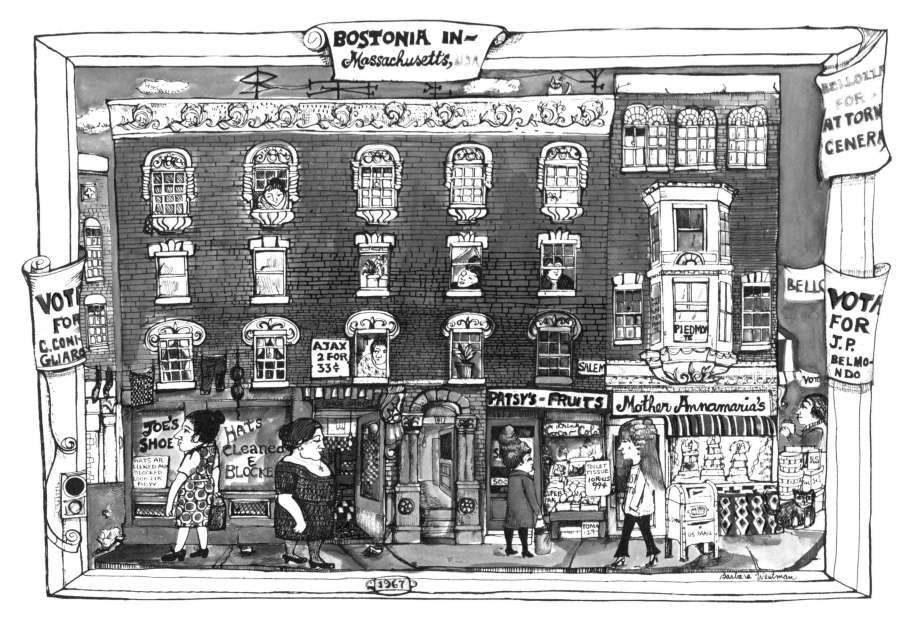

This is a made up picture. I saw a cat somewhere and those
people somewhere and put them together one night at home.

Lanterns were hung
in the steeple of this church
April 18, 1775,
to warn the people the
British troops were marching
on Lexington and Concord.

CHRIST CHURCH 1723 BOSTON

Paul Revere was HERE they say – very early

He swung his lantern with all his might and saved his country from a terrible Fright

This Church is in the North End.

Actually a man name of Robert Newman was the real swinger of the lantern. Paul Revere did the riding. He was very Brave as He took messages to Concord and Lexington By horse. That was a Long way by horse. He was very Brave. It was a tough job and he did it well.

Barbara Westman was here

Prato means "meadow" in Italian. This meadow of bricks
leads to the Old North Church. It is a place where the men and women talk
and the children play, and a fountain sparkles all day long.

**This is Hanover Street in the North End
with St. Stephen's Church in the background.**

Next pages: **This view of the Charles River from the
Science Museum shows the "salt and pepper shaker" bridge.**

One great thing about Boston — you can walk right to the edge of it.

Barbara Westman

FRANKLIN PIERCE COLLEGE LIBRARY

00079674

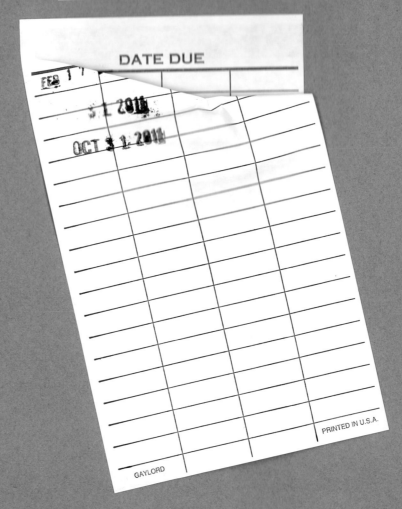

DATE DUE

FEB 1 7			
3 1 2011			
OCT 3 1 2011			
			PRINTED IN U.S.A.
GAYLORD			